KINGFISHER
READERS

level
4

D0381876

Flight

Chris Oxlade

KINGFISHER

KINGFISHER

First published 2012 by Kingfisher
an imprint of Macmillan Children's Books
a division of Macmillan Publishers Limited
20 New Wharf Road, London N1 9RR
Basingstoke and Oxford
Associated companies throughout the world
www.panmacmillan.com

Series editor: Heather Morris
Literacy consultant: Hilary Horton
Flight consultant: Andrew Nahun

ISBN: 978-0-7534-3064-4
Copyright © Macmillan Publishers Ltd 2012

9 8 7 6 5 4 3 2 1

1TR/1011/WKT/UNTD/105MA

A CIP catalogue record for this book is available from
the British Library.

Printed in China

Picture credits

The Publisher would like to thank the following for permission to reproduce their material. Every care has
been taken to trace copyright holders. However, if there have been unintentional omissions or failure to trace
copyright holders, we apologize and will, if informed, endeavour to make corrections in any future edition
(t = top, c = centre, r = right, l = left):

Cover Shutterstock/Takahashi Photography; Shutterstock/David Brimm; Pages 4–5 Photolibrary/age foto;
5t Shutterstock/MarchCattle; 5b Shutterstock/Mircea Bezergheanu; 6 Photolibrary/corbis; 7 Shutterstock/
IDesign; 8t Frank Lane Picture Agency (FLPA)/Jef Meul; 8b Alamy/WaterFrame; 9 FLPA/Michael Durham/
Minden; 10 Alamy/MEPL; 11t Alamy/The Art Archive; 12 Science Photo Libraru (SPL)/Science Source;
13t Alamy/Todd Muskopf; 13b SPL/US Library of Congress; 15 Shutterstock/Ivan Cholakov Gostock-dot-net;
16 Shutterstock/Paul Drabot; 17b Shutterstock/Ramon Berk; 18 Shutterstock/Carlos E. Santa Maria;
19b Shutterstock/Oleg Yarko; 20 Alamy/Nick Servian; 21t Photolibrary/Corbis; 21b Alamy/Antony Nettle;
22 Shutterstock/Yves Smolders; 23t Shutterstock/Gabriel Nardelli Araujo; 23b Alamy/Andi Duff;
24 Shutterstock/David Brimm; 26 Shutterstock/Uwe Bumann; 27t Shutterstock/Gary Blakeley; 27b Corbis;
29 Photolibrary/Pure Stock; 29 Corbis; all other images from the Kingfisher Artbank.

Contents

Flight and flying

What do birds, bats, planes and kites have in common? They all fly! Flight is travelling through the air. In this book, you can find out about all sorts of things that fly, from butterflies and bats to helicopters and space rockets.

Birds fly to find food for themselves and their young. They also take off to escape from **predators**, such as foxes.

This **airliner** is full of passengers taking off at the start of a flight.

Kite flying

A kite is a very simple flying machine. The wind lifts the kite into the air. Pulling the strings makes it swoop through the air. Kites come in all sorts of shapes and sizes.

Birds in flight

Birds make flying look easy as they dive and swoop through the air. A bird flies with its **wings**. The wings lift the bird into the air and push the bird along. They are made of large feathers, called flight feathers. The wings have a curved shape. When a bird is flying, air goes over and under the wings.
This lifts the bird.

Bones: A bird's bones are very strong, but they are also very light.

Muscles: A bird has strong muscles that flap its wings.

Tail: A bird uses the feathers on its tail to steer and to slow down.

Did you know?

The albatross has the longest wings of any bird. The distance from the tip of one wing to the tip of the other wing can be 3.4 metres — that's the same length as two adults lying head to toe.

This tiny hummingbird flaps its wings so fast that the wings make a humming noise. It is drinking **nectar** from a flower.

Flapping and soaring

Small birds, like starlings and robins, flap their wings fast to keep flying. Bigger birds, like eagles and gulls, do lots of **gliding**. They fly with their wings spread out wide. Flying like this is called soaring.

More flying animals

Bees, flies, butterflies and dragonflies are all
insects that fly. Insects fly to look for food.
Small flying insects, like bees and wasps, flap
their tiny wings very fast. Their flapping wings
make the buzzing sound you hear when they
fly near you.

Flying fish

Flying fish leap out of the water
to escape from predators. They
spread out their fins like wings,
and glide through the air.

Bats are animals with wings covered by skin. Most bats are nocturnal, which means they sleep in the daytime and fly at night. Bats make sounds as they fly, and they listen for the sounds to bounce back off things. This is how they catch flying insects such as moths. Humans can't hear the sounds that bats make.

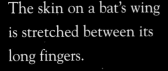

The skin on a bat's wing is stretched between its long fingers.

Trying to fly

People wanted to fly a long time before **aircraft** were invented. They saw birds flying by and wanted to copy them. But they didn't understand how birds flew.

Some people made wings that looked like bird wings. They put them on their arms and jumped from tall towers. But their arms were not strong enough to flap the wings and they fell to the ground.

The story of Icarus

In a story from ancient Greece, a boy called Icarus flew with wings made of wax and feathers. But when he flew too close to the Sun, the wax melted and Icarus fell to Earth.

The first time people flew was in a balloon, in the year 1783. Two French brothers, called the Montgolfiers, made the balloon. A fire heated the air inside the balloon, which made the balloon float up.

The Montgolfiers' balloon was made from paper and was brightly painted.

In 1890, a French inventor called Clement Ader built a plane that looked like a box with giant bat wings. It had a steam engine and a giant propeller.

Clement Ader's plane only managed a short hop of about 50 metres.

The first plane

In the year 1903, a very famous flight happened. It was the first time a plane with an engine flew into the air. The plane was called *Flyer*, and it was built by two American brothers, Wilbur and Orville Wright.

The Wright brothers did lots of careful experiments with kites and **gliders**. They worked out how to make wings, how to make a plane climb, descend, and turn left and right. Then they built *Flyer*.

Orville Wright at the controls of one of the Wright brothers' planes.

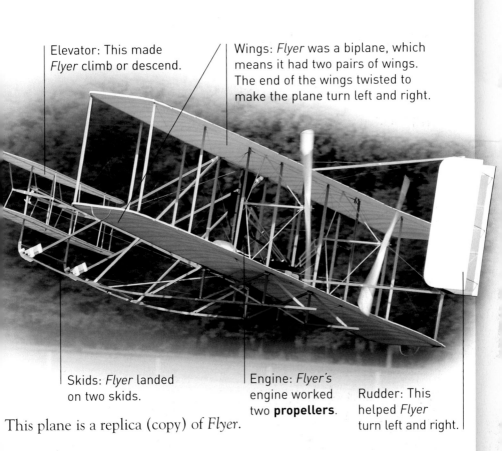

Elevator: This made *Flyer* climb or descend.

Wings: *Flyer* was a biplane, which means it had two pairs of wings. The end of the wings twisted to make the plane turn left and right.

Skids: *Flyer* landed on two skids.

Engine: *Flyer's* engine worked two **propellers**.

Rudder: This helped *Flyer* turn left and right.

This plane is a replica (copy) of *Flyer*.

A famous flight

Orville Wright was the pilot when *Flyer* took off for the first time. His brother Wilbur held his breath as he watched *Flyer* speed along the ground and into the air. The flight only lasted a few seconds, but *Flyer* worked!

13

Modern planes

Modern planes look very different from the planes the Wright brothers flew. The body of a plane is called the **fuselage**. The fuselage is a long tube made of metal. Passengers or cargo go in the fuselage. The **pilot** sits in the **cockpit**, which is at the front of the fuselage.

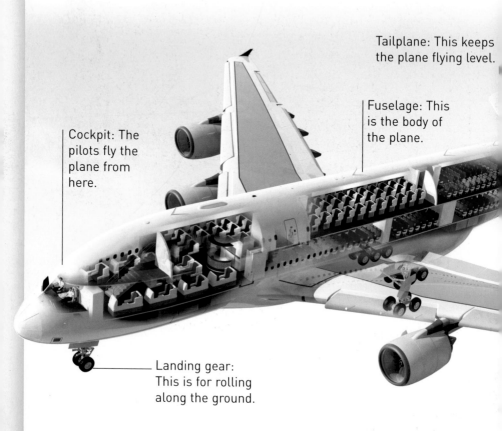

Tailplane: This keeps the plane flying level.

Fuselage: This is the body of the plane.

Cockpit: The pilots fly the plane from here.

Landing gear: This is for rolling along the ground.

Flying forces

This picture shows the pushes and pulls on a plane when it is flying. These pushes and pulls are called forces.

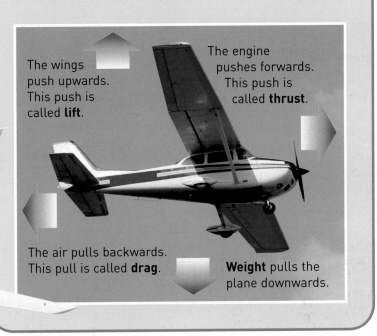

The wings push upwards. This push is called **lift**.

The engine pushes forwards. This push is called **thrust**.

The air pulls backwards. This pull is called **drag**.

Weight pulls the plane downwards.

Fin: This keeps the plane flying in a straight line.

Wings: These lift the plane into the air. They only work when the plane is travelling fast enough. If a plane flies too slowly, the wings stop lifting it.

Engine: This pushes the plane through the air.

Plane engines

Engines push planes along. Small planes and slow planes have propeller engines. These engines make a propeller spin very fast, like a giant fan. The propeller pushes on the air, which pushes the plane along.

Most large planes and very fast planes have jet engines. These engines don't have propellers. They make a stream of gas instead.

You can see the exhaust from this fighter plane's two jet engines.

Inside a jet engine, spinning blades squeeze the air. Then the air is mixed with fuel. The fuel burns. This makes lots of hot gas, which roars out of the engine's **exhaust**. The gas shoots backwards and pushes the plane forwards.

Turbine: The gas spins the turbine, and the turbine works the fan.

Exhaust: The jet of gases comes out here.

Burners: The fuel burns in here.

Fan: This sucks air into the engine and squeezes it.

Did you know?

The biggest jet engine ever made is the General Electric GE90. Its fan is an amazing 3.25 metres across. This engine was built specially for an airliner called the Boeing 777. There are two of these engines on the Boeing 777.

Flying a plane

A plane's cockpit is full of handles, pedals, switches and dials. A pilot steers with a stick called the control column and two pedals.

The control column and the pedals make the plane climb upwards, descend, turn left and right, and roll from side to side. A handle called the throttle makes the engines go faster or slower.

Steering a plane

The control column moves the ailerons on the wings and the elevators on the tailplane. The pedals make the rudder move from side to side.

Elevators are on the tailplane. They tip up or down together. They make the plane's nose go up or down.

The rudder is on the fin. It makes the plane turn from side to side.

Ailerons are on the wings. One tips up when the other tips down. They make the plane roll from side to side.

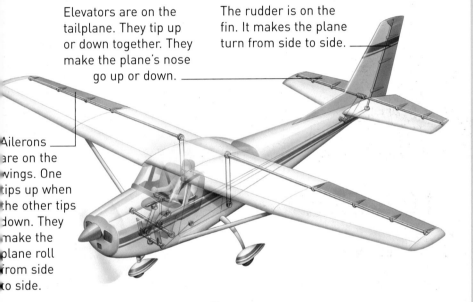

Planes with no pilots

Many planes have an autopilot. This is a computer that flies a plane automatically so the pilot can rest. **Spy planes** like this one don't need a pilot at all. People fly them by remote control.

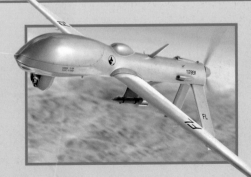

19

Take-off and landing

Take-off is when a plane lifts off the ground. Planes take off from a long, flat area called a **runway**. The pilot steers the plane to the end of the runway, ready for take-off. Then the pilot puts the engines on full power and the plane rolls forwards. It gets faster and faster until it lifts into the air.

Planes must be moving fast along the ground before they can take off.

This airliner is about to land.

At the end of a flight, a plane lands on a runway, too. This is the most difficult part of a flight for the pilot. The pilot slows down the plane and puts down the **landing gear**. As soon as the plane's wheels touch the runway, the engines go into reverse. This quickly stops the plane.

Vertical take-off

Some planes don't need a runway because they take off upwards instead of forwards. The exhausts of a plane's engines point downwards for a vertical take-off.

Planes that take off vertically, like this F-35 fighter, are used on ships called aircraft carriers.

Gliders

A glider is a plane that doesn't have engines. Gliders need help to take off. A plane with an engine tows a glider into the air on a long rope. When the glider is high up, the plane lets it go. Then the glider glides gently back to the ground.

Gliders have long, thin wings, which help them stay in the air for as long as they can.

This is a paraglider. The pilot pulls the strings to steer.

Some gliders don't look like planes at all. A hang-glider has just a wing. The pilot hangs underneath. A paraglider looks like a kite or a parachute. The kite fills with air as it flies along.

Gliding in a suit

This **skydiver** is wearing a gliding suit. It has small wings on each side. The skydiver spreads his arms and legs to glide down through the air.

Helicopters

Chop, chop, chop, chop... it's the sound of a helicopter flying close by. The sound comes from the helicopter's **rotor**. The rotor spins round very fast and lifts the helicopter into the air. A helicopter doesn't need a runway to take off or land. It goes straight up and comes straight down.

Rotor blades: When the rotor spins, the blades lift the helicopter upwards.

Rotor: This makes the blades spin round.

Engine: This makes the rotor spin round.

Tail rotor: This stops the fuselage spinning round.

Fuselage: This is the space for passengers and cargo.

This rescue helicopter is lifting a man from the sea.

Did you know?
The biggest helicopter ever made was called the Mil V-12 and it was made in the 1960s. It had two giant rotors side by side and could carry 40 tonnes of cargo.

Helicopters work where there are no runways. Passenger helicopters can land in small spaces in cities, and even on the tops of buildings. Armies use transport helicopters to move soldiers and their equipment. Rescue helicopters help people who are in trouble at sea or in the mountains.

Jobs planes do

Planes do lots of different jobs. Most planes are passenger planes. Large passenger planes carry hundreds of people for thousands of kilometres without stopping. Cargo planes carry things from place to place. Inside a cargo plane's fuselage is a huge empty space, ready to be filled with goods, packages and parcels.

Workers loading a cargo plane

Did you know?

The biggest airliner in the world is the Airbus A380. It is a double-decker plane and is 73 metres long. It can carry 853 passengers.

This fire-fighting plane is dropping its load of water.

Some planes do special jobs. There are planes that fight forest fires, planes that work as flying ambulances, planes that carry fuel for other planes, and planes that farmers use to spray their crops.

A fighter plane getting fuel from a tanker plane

Space flight

Three... two... one... we have lift off!
A rocket is beginning its journey. Rockets
carry astronauts and cargo into space.

A rocket has an
engine that pushes
it upwards and into
space. Fuel burns
inside the engine and
makes hot gases. The
gases blast out of the
engine and push the
rocket upwards.

After lift-off, the
rocket goes faster and
faster. After a few
minutes it is in orbit,
flying round and
round the Earth.

SpaceShipTwo is a new spacecraft. It will soon carry tourists into space. A jet plane called WhiteKnightTwo carries it into the air. Then the pilot turns on the rocket engine and the spacecraft flies into space. After a few minutes it glides back to Earth.

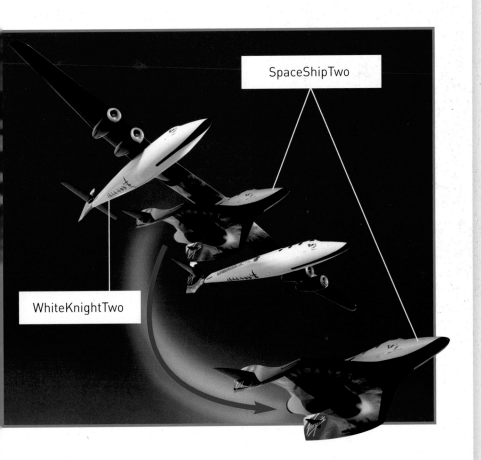

SpaceShipTwo

WhiteKnightTwo

This picture shows SpaceShipTwo leaving WhiteKnightTwo on its way to space.

Glossary

aircraft A machine that flies.

airliner A large plane that carries passengers.

climb To fly upwards.

cockpit The space in a plane where the pilot sits.

descend To fly downwards.

drag A push from the air that slows down a plane.

engine A machine that pushes a plane along.

exhaust Where gases come out of an engine.

fuselage The body of a plane, shaped like a tube.

glider A plane with no engine.

gliding Flying without moving wings (bird) or using an engine (plane).

insect A minibeast with six legs and a hard case around its body.

landing gear Aircraft wheels used for landing, take-off and moving on the ground.

lift An upwards push made by a plane's wings.

nectar A sweet liquid that flowers make to attract insects and birds.

pilot A person who flies a plane.

predator An animal that eats other animals.

propeller An object like a fan that is turned by a plane's engine. It pushes a plane along.

rotor Part of a machine that spins round very fast.

runway A long, wide area where planes take off and land.

skydiver A person who jumps from a plane and lands using a parachute.

spy plane A plane that flies high in the sky and photographs the ground below.

thrust The push made by a plane's engines.

weight The pull made by gravity that makes things fall to the ground.

wings The parts of a plane or a flying animal that lift the plane or animal into the air.

Index